U.S. Citizenship
Test Practice
(Chinese – English) 2018 - 2019
100 Bilingual Civics Questions (中文 · 英文)
plus Flashcards, USCIS Vocabulary,
and More

Lakewood Publishing

U.S. Citizenship Test Practice
(Chinese – English) 2018 - 2019
100 Bilingual Civics Questions (中文 · 英文)
plus Flashcards, USCIS Vocabulary, and More

ISBN: 978-1-936583-54-6
Copyright © 2018 by Lakewood Publishing

Published by Lakewood Publishing
275 E. Hillcrest Ave., #160 Ste. 213
Thousand Oaks, CA 91360
1. Citizenship, United States, America, U.S. 2. naturalization, citizenship
3. immigration, citizenship test, new test
4 Chinese – language 5. Mandarin - language 6. English - language
7. bilingual – language
9. United States – civics, government
9. United States – USCIS citizenship test September 2018
I. Citizenship, American   II. Title

U.S. Citizenship Test Practice Chinese - English 2018 - 2019
中文・英文

100 Bilingual Questions and Answers
公民入籍歸化考試的100道考題與答案
plus Practice Quiz, Flashcards, USCIS
Reading and Writing Vocabulary,
and More

For Civics and Citizenship
www.lakewoodpublishing.com

Learn About the United States: 100 Civics Questions with Short Readings and More for the New USCIS CitizenshipTest
ISBN 978-1-936583-57-7
ISBN 978-1-936583-62-1 (ebook)

U.S. Citizenship Test Series: Multilingual

U.S. Citizenship Test Practice (English) 2018 - 2019
100 Civics Questions, plus Flashcards, USCIS Vocabulary and More
ISBN 978-1-936583-52-2

U.S. Citizenship Test Practice (Spanish – English) 2018 - 2019
100 Bilingual Civics Questions (Español • Inglés), plus Flashcards, USCIS Vocabulary and More
ISBN 978-1-936583-53-9
100 Preguntas y Respuestas para el Examen de E.U. Ciudadanía

U.S. Citizenship Test Practice (Chinese – English) 2018 - 2019
100 Bilingual Civics Questions (中文• 英文) plus Flashcards, USCIS Vocabulary, and More
ISBN: 978-1-936583-54-6
公民入籍歸化考試的100道考題與答案

U.S. Citizenship Test Practice (Korean – English) 2018 - 2019
100 Bilingual Civics Questions (한국어 • 영어), plus Flashcards, USCIS Vocabulary, and More
ISBN 978-1-936583-55-3   미국시민권시험인터뷰질문

U.S. Citizenship Test Practice (Vietnamese – English) 2018 - 2019
100 Bilingual Civics Questions (tiếng Việt • tiếng Anh), plus Flashcards, USCIS Vocabulary, and More
ISBN 978-1-936583-56-0
100 câu hỏi và câu trả lời để chuẩn bị cho kỳ thi quốc tich Mỹ

General Interest

Surviving Disasters: From Earthquakes and Fires to Hurricanes and Terrorism
ISBN 978-1-936583-63-8
ISBN 978-1-936583-64-5 (ebook)

THE ELEMENTS OF STYLE* 18 Essential Rules for Good Writing in English (*Strunk's original; newly formatted)
ISBN 978-1-936583-36-2

The Jefferson Bible: What Thomas Jefferson Selected as the Life and Morals of Jesus of Nazareth
ISBN 978-1-936583-21-8
ISBN 978-1-936583-22-5 (hardcover)
ISBN 978-1-936583-27-0 (ebook)

The DASH Diet Solution and 60 Day Weight Loss and Fitness Journal
ISBN 978-1-936583-29-4
ISBN 978-1-936583-28-7 (hardcover)

How-To Guides for Immigrants Living in the United States (in English or in Spanish)

A Guide for New Immigrants to the United States: What Everyone Should Know
ISBN 978-1-936583-58-4

Un guía para inmigrantes nuevos a los Estados Unidos: lo que deben saber
ISBN 978-1-936583-59-1

您考慮入籍美國嗎？

永久居民擁有美國公民大多數的權利。然而，
還有許多重要的原因讓您考慮入籍 美國。成為公民後，
您將被賦予所有的公民權利。同時， 您也接受了作為美國公
民的全部責任。公民身份為我和我的家人開拓了更多更好的
機會
我選擇機會。我選擇成為美國公民。

◆

Do You Want to Become a U.S. Citizen?

Permanent residents have most of the rights of U.S.
citizens. However, there are many important reasons to
consider U.S. citizenship. When you become a citizen,
you will receive all the rights of citizenship. You also
accept all of the responsibilities of being an American.
"I choose to become a U.S. citizen."
https://www.uscis.gov

目錄・**Contents**

I
中文・英文
Chinese・English

II
English

您符合申請入籍美國的資格嗎？

在一般情況下，您必須符合以下要求:
年滿18歲。
能夠讀, 寫及講基本英語。
對美國歷史和政府（公民知識）具基本了解。
品格良好。 對美國憲法的原則和理念表示認同。
*擁有永久居民身份至少5年。
*已連續定居美國至少5年。
*證明實際居留　美國至少30個月。
*證明已在申請入籍所在地或移民局的轄區居住至少3個月。

* 如果您已經與一名美國公民結婚，　此項要求可能會改變。

Are You Ready to Apply for U.S. Citizenship?

In general, you must meet the following requirements:
Be at least 18 years old.

Be able to read, write, and speak basic English.

Have a basic understanding of U.S. history and government (civics).

Be a person of good moral character.

Demonstrate an attachment to the principles and ideals of the U.S. Constitution.

*Be a permanent resident for at least 5 years.

*Demonstrate continuous permanent residence in the United States for at least 5 years.

*Prove you have been physically present in the U.S.for 30 months.

*Show that you have lived for at least 3 months in the state or USCIS district where you apply.

* This requirement may change if you are married to a U.S. citizen.　https://www.uscis.gov

I

中文・英文
Chinese - English

Note: The answer to Question #47—"What is the name of the Speaker of the House?"— will change in January 2019. To learn about the new Speaker in 2019, go to www.lakewoodpublishing.com.

第47號問題的答案 - 眾議院議長的名字 - 將於2019年1月發生變化。請訪問 www.lakewoodpublishing.com 了解新議長。

公民（歷史與政府）歸化試題

以下所列為公民（歷史與政府的）歸化的 100
道試題與答案。公民測驗是口試，由 USCIS
主考官向申請人提問 100 道公民試題中的 10
道。申請人必須從 10 道中正確回答 6
道才能通過入籍歸化的公民測驗部分。

在公民入籍考試中，有些問題的答案會因選舉或任命結果而
改變。當您學習考題時，請務必確定您知道該類試題的最新
答案。當您到美國公民及移民服務局（USCIS）接受公民入籍
面試時，您需要回答當時在位任職的政府官員之姓名。美國
公民及移民服務局的面試官將不會認可錯誤的答案。
USCIS瞭解這 100
道試題可能有額外的正確答案，但是我們建議申請人回答公
民測驗試題時用以下提供的答案。

6, 11, 13, 17, 20, 27, 28, 44, 45, 49, 54, 56, 70, 75, 78,
85, 94, 95, 97, 99

Introduction to the Civics Test Questions

USCIS Civics Questions for the
New 2018 Naturalization Test

Becoming an American citizen is one of the most important decisions that you can make. If you meet the requirements for citizenship (pg 8), you need to complete the application, Form N-400. Then USCIS will schedule your naturalization interview for citizenship.

At the interview, you need to show you can read, write, and speak English. You also need to know the answers to 100 civics questions. The USCIS officer will ask you up to 10 of the 100 civics questions in this book and you will answer orally. You will not need to read or write any of your answers for the civics test.

You will not know which ten questions the interviewer will ask you, but they will all be chosen from the questions in this book. You must answer 6 out of 10 questions correctly to pass the civics part of the naturalization test.

There may be other correct answers to the 100 civics questions, but you should give the USCIS answer.

The USCIS interviewer will also talk with you to see that you can understand and speak basic English. Many of the questions will be about the information on your N-400 form.

You will also need to show that you can read and write basic English. The USCIS lists of words you need to know for this are also included in this book, beginning on page 111.

65/20

If you are 65 years old or older and have been a legal permanent resident of the United States for 20 years or more, you only need to know the answers to the 20 questions that have been marked with an asterisk.

Chapter 3 lists these questions separately for people over 65 years old. They begin on page 71.

公民入籍歸化考試的100道考題與答案

100 Civics Questions and Answers

公民入籍歸化考試的100道考題與答案

A: 美國民主原則

1. 美國的最高法律是什麼？

   ▪ 憲法

2. 憲法的作用是什麼？

   ▪ 建立政府體制
   ▪ 定義政府
   ▪ 保護美國人的基本權利

3. 憲法的前三個字說明自治的概念. 這三個字是什麼？

   ▪ 我們人民

4. 什麼是修正案？

   ▪ （憲法的）更正
   ▪ （憲法的）補充

5. 憲法的前十項修正案稱為什麼？

   ▪ 權利法案

100 Civics Questions and Answers

A: Principles of American Democracy

1. What is the supreme law of the land?

the Constitution

2. What does the Constitution do? (All answers below are correct. Know <u>one</u> for the test.)

- sets up the government
- defines the government
- protects basic rights of Americans

3. The idea of self-government is in the first three words of the Constitution. What are these words?

We the People

4. What is an amendment? (Know <u>one</u> way to say it)

- a change (to the Constitution)
- an addition (to the Constitution)

5. What do we call the first ten amendments to the Constitution?

The Bill of Rights

*6. 列舉憲法第一條修正案中的一項權利或自由？

- 言論自由
- 宗教自由
- 集會結社的自由
- 出版自由
- 向政府請願的自由

7. 憲法有幾條修正案？

- 二十七 (27) 條

8.「獨立宣言」的作用是什麼？

- 宣佈美國（脫離英國而）獨立
- 宣告美國（脫離英國而）獨立
- 表示美國（脫離英國而）獨立

9. 列舉「獨立宣言」中的兩項權利？

- 生命（的權利）
- 自由（的權利）
- 追求幸福（的權利）

*6. What is <u>one</u> right or freedom given in the First Amendment?

- speech
- religion
- assembly
- press
- petition the government

7. How many amendments does the U.S. Constitution have?

twenty-seven (27)

8. What did the Declaration of Independence do? (Know <u>one</u> answer for the citizenship test.)

- announced our independence (from Great Britain)
- declared our independence (from Great Britain)
- said that the United States is free (from Great Britain)

9. What are <u>two</u> rights in the Declaration of Independence? (All are correct. Know two.)

- life
- liberty
- the pursuit of happiness

10. 什麼是宗教自由？

   ▪ 你可以信仰任何宗教，也可以不信仰任何宗教.

*11. 美國的經濟制度是什麼？

   ▪ 資本主義經濟
   ▪ 市場經濟

12. 「法治」是什麼？

   ▪ 人人都應遵守法律.
   ▪ 領導人必須遵守法律.
   ▪ 政府必須遵守法律.
   ▪ 沒有任何人在法律之上.

B: 政治體制

*13. 列舉政府體制的一個分支或部門.

   ▪ 立法部門（國會）
   ▪ 行政部門（總統）
   ▪ 司法部門（法院）

10. What is freedom of religion?

>You can practice any religion, or not
>practice (have) a religion.

*11. What is the economic system in the United
States? (Know one of these ways to say it.)

>- capitalist economy
>- market economy

12. What is the "rule of law"? (Know <u>one</u> of
these answers for the test.)

>- Everyone must follow the law.
>- Leaders must obey the law.
>- Government must obey the law.
>- No one is above the law.

B: The U.S. System of Government

*13. Name <u>one</u> branch or part of the
government.

>- legislative bramch (the Congress)
>- executive branch (the President)
>- judicial branch (the courts)

14. 什麼防止一個政府分支變得過於強大？

- 制衡 +
- 權力分立

15. 誰負責行政部門？

- 總統

16. 誰制定聯邦法律？

- 國會
- 參議院及眾議院
- （美國或國家）立法部門

*17. 美國國會由哪兩個部分組成？

- 參議院與眾議院

18. 美國參議員有幾位？

- 一百 (100) 位

14. What stops one branch of government from becoming too powerful? (There are two ways to say it. Know one).

- checks and balances
- separation of powers

15. Who is in charge of the executive branch?

- the President

16. Who makes federal laws? (All are correct ways to say the same answer. Know one.)

- Congress
- Senate and House (of Representatives)
- (U.S. or national) legislature

*17. What are the two parts of the U.S. Congress?

- the Senate and the House of Representatives

18. How many U.S. senators are there?

one hundred (100)

19. 我們選出的美國參議員任職多少年？

　　▪ 六 (6) 年

*20. 您所在州的現任一位美國參議員的名字是什麼？

　　▪ 答案依所在州不同而異　．
　　〔住在哥倫比亞特區和美國領
　　土的居民可答:哥倫比亞特區當地
　　(或應試居民所在領地)沒有美國參議員 .)

21. 眾議院中有投票權的眾議員有幾位？

　　▪ 四百三十五 (435) 位

22. 我們選出的美國眾議員任職多少年？

　　▪ 兩 (2) 年

23. 列舉您所在選區的美國眾議員的名字 .

　　▪ 答案依所在州不同而異
〔住在沒有投票權的美國領地當地代表或專員之應試者可以
　　說明當地代表或專員的姓名 .
　　說明自己選區沒有國會（投票）代表也是可接受的答案 .〕

19. We elect a U.S. senator for how many years in each term?

- six (6)

*20. Who is one of your state's U.S. senators now?

My senator is: _____'

▪ Answers will be different for each state. Check the internet **www.senate.gov** for the current senators in your state. [People who live in the District of Columbia or a U.S. territory should answer that they have no U.S. senators.]

21. The House of Representatives has how many voting members?

- four hundred thirty-five (435)

22. We elect a U.S. representative for how many years?

- two (2)

23. Name your U.S. representative.

My U.S. Representative is: _____

▪ Answers will be different for each area. See the website: **www.house.gov** for the newest names. [Residents of territories—not states—can say that "the territory has no (voting) Representatives in Congress".]

24. 美國參議員代表何人？

  ▪ 其所在州的所有人民

25. 為什麼有些州的眾議員人數比其他州多？

  ▪ （由於）該州的人口
  ▪ （由於）該州有更多人口
  ▪ （由於）該州的人口比其他州多

26. 我們選出的總統任職多少年？

  ▪ 四 (4) 年

*27. 我們在哪一個月選總統？

  ▪ 十一月

*28. 現任美國總統的名字是什麼？

  ▪ Trump
  ▪ Donald Trump

29. 現任美國副總統的名字是什麼？

  ▪ Pence
  ▪ Mike Pence

24. Who does a U.S. senator represent?

all the people of the state

25. Why do some states have more Representatives than other states? (Know one way to say it. All are correct)

- (because) some states have more people and so they get more representatives
- (because of) the state's population
- (because) they have more people

26. We elect a President for how many years?

- four (4)

*27. In what month do we vote for President?

- November

*28. What is the name of the President of the United States now? (Both ways are correct.)

- Trump
- Donald Trump

29. What is the name of the Vice President of the United States now? (Both ways to say it are correct)

- Pence
- Mike Pence

30. 如果總統不能視事, 則由誰成為總統？

- 副總統

31. 如果總統和副總統都不能視事, 則由誰成為總統？

- 眾議院議長

32. 誰是三軍統帥？

- 總統

33. 誰簽署法案使之成為法律？

- 總統

34. 誰否決法案？

- 總統

35. 總統的內閣做什麼事？

- 向總統提出建議

The U.S. Constitution

30. If the President can no longer serve, who becomes President?

   - the Vice President

31. If both the President and the Vice President can no longer serve, who becomes President?

   - the Speaker of the House

32. Who is the Commander-in-Chief of the military?

   - the President

33. Who signs bills to become laws?

   - the President

34. Who vetoes bills?

   - the President

35. What does the President's Cabinet do?

   - It advises the President

36. <u>兩個</u>內閣級別的職位是什麼？

- 農業部長
- 商務部長
- 國防部長
- 教育部長
- 能源部長
- 健康與人類服務部長
- 國土安全部長
- 住宅與都市發展部長
- 內政部長
- 勞工部長
- 國務卿
- 交通部長
- 財政部長
- 退伍軍人事務部長
- 司法部長
- 副總統

37. 司法部門做什麼？

- 審查法律
- 解釋法律
- 解決爭議（意見不一致）
- 決定某一法律是否牴觸憲法

36. What are two Cabinet-level positions?

- Vice President
- Attorney General
- Secretary of Agriculture
- Secretary of Commerce
- Secretary of Defense
- Secretary of Education
- Secretary of Energy
- Secretary of Health and Human Services
- Secretary of Homeland Security
- Secretary of Housing and Urban
    Development
- Secretary of the Interior
- Secretary of Labor
- Secretary of State
- Secretary of Transportation
- Secretary of the Treasury
- Secretary of Veterans Affairs

37. What does the judicial branch do? (Know one answer for naturalization.)

- reviews laws
- explains laws
- resolves disputes (disagreements)
- decides if a law goes against the
    Constitution

38. 美國最高法院是什麼？

- 聯邦最高法院

39. 最高法院有幾位大法官？

- 九 **(9)** 位

Chief Justice John Roberts
Official Supreme Court Portrait

40. 現任聯邦首席大法官是誰？

- 約翰・羅伯茲（小約翰 **G.** 羅伯茲）

41. 根據我國憲法. 有些權力屬於聯邦政府.
聯邦政府的一項權力是什麼？

- 印製鈔票
- 宣戰
- 創立軍隊
- 簽訂條約

38. What is the highest court in the United States?

   - the Supreme Court

39. How many justices are on the Supreme Court?

   - nine (9)

40. Who is the Chief Justice of the United States now?

   - John Roberts

41. Under our Constitution, some powers belong to the federal government. What is <u>one</u> power of the federal government?

   - to print money
   - to declare war
   - to make treaties
   - to create an army

President Donald Trump
Official White House Photo

42. 根據我國憲法, 有些權力屬於州政府.
州政府的一項權力是什麼?

- 提供教育
- 提供保護（警員）
- 提供安全（消防局）
- 提供駕駛執照
- 批准區劃與土地使用

43. 您居住州的現任州長是誰?

- 答案依居住州不同而異. 〔哥倫比亞特區的居民應回答:我們沒有州長.〕

Vice President Mike Pence
Official White House Photo

42. Under our Constitution, some powers belong to the states. What is <u>one</u> power of the states? (All are correct.)

- provide schooling and education
- provide protection (police)
- provide safety (fire departments)
- give a driver's license
- approve zoning and land use

43. Who is the Governor of your state now?

The governor is _____

▪ Answers will be different for each state. If you don't know, ask at the public library. [District of Columbia residents should answer that D.C. does not have a governor]

*44. 您居住州的首府是哪裡？

▪ 答案依居住州不同而異.〔哥倫比亞特區居民應回答哥倫比亞特區不是一個州, 沒有首府. 美國領地居民應回答居住領地的首府.〕

Alabama - Montgomery

Alaska - Juneau

Arizona - Phoenix

Arkansas - Little Rock

California -Sacramento

Colorado - Denver

Connecticut -Hartford

Delaware - Dover

Florida - Tallahassee

Georgia - Atlanta

Hawaii - Honolulu

Idaho - Boise

Illinois - Springfield

Indiana - Indianapolis

Iowa - Des Moines

Kansas - Topeka

Kentucky - Frankfort

Louisiana - Baton Rouge

Maine - Augusta

Maryland - Annapolis

Massachusetts - Boston

Michigan - Lansing

Minnesota - St. Paul

Mississippi - Jackson

Missouri - Jefferson City

Montana - Helena

Nebraska - Lincoln

Nevada - Carson City

New Hampshire - Concord

New Jersey - Trenton

New Mexico - Santa Fe

New York - Albany

North Carolina – Raleigh

North Dakota - Bismarck

Ohio - Columbus

Oklahoma - Oklahoma City

Oregon - Salem

Pennsylvania - Harrisburg

Rhode Island - Providence

South Carolina - Columbia

South Dakota - Pierre

Tennessee - Nashville

Texas - Austin

Utah - Salt Lake City

Vermont - Montpelier

Virginia - Richmond

Washington - Olympia

West Virginia - Charleston

Wisconsin - Madison

Wyoming - Cheyenne

*44. What is the capital of your state?

[People who live in the District of Columbia should answer that D.C. is not a state and does not have a capital. Residents of U.S. territories should name the capital of the territory.]

The States and the State Capitals

Alabama - Montgomery
Alaska - Juneau
Arizona - Phoenix
Arkansas - Little Rock
California - Sacramento
Colorado - Denver
Connecticut - Hartford
Delaware - Dover
Florida - Tallahassee
Georgia - Atlanta
Hawaii - Honolulu
Idaho - Boise
Illinois - Springfield
Indiana - Indianapolis
Iowa - Des Moines
Kansas - Topeka
Kentucky - Frankfort
Louisiana - Baton Rouge
Maine - Augusta
Maryland - Annapolis
Massachusetts - Boston
Michigan - Lansing
Minnesota - St. Paul
Mississippi - Jackson
Missouri - Jefferson City

Montana - Helena
Nebraska - Lincoln
Nevada - Carson City
New Hampshire - Concord
New Jersey - Trenton
New Mexico - Santa Fe
New York - Albany
North Carolina – Raleigh
North Dakota – Bismarck
Ohio - Columbus
Oklahoma - Oklahoma City
Oregon - Salem
Pennsylvania - Harrisburg
Rhode Island - Providence
South Carolina - Columbia
South Dakota - Pierre
Tennessee - Nashville
Texas - Austin
Utah - Salt Lake City
Vermont - Montpelier
Virginia - Richmond
Washington - Olympia
West Virginia - Charleston
Wisconsin - Madison
Wyoming - Cheyenne

*45. 美國當今兩大政黨為何？

- 民主黨與共和黨

46. 現任總統屬於哪個政黨？

- 民主黨

47. 現任國會眾議院議長的名字是什麼？

- （南茜）波洛西（这将改变2019年1月）

C: 權利與責任

48. 憲法中有四個關於誰可以投票的修正案. 試舉一個.

- 十八 *(18)* 歲以上的公民（可以投票）.
- 您投票不必繳錢（繳投票稅）.
- 任何公民都可以投票（男性與女性都可以投票）.
- 任何種族的男性公民（都可以投票）.

*49. 列舉一項美國公民才有的責任？

- 當陪審員
- 在聯邦選舉中投票

*45. What are the two major political parties
in the United States?

 - Democratic and Republican

46. What is the political party of the President
now?

 - the Republican (Party)

47. What is the name of the Speaker of the
House of Representatives now?

 - Paul Ryan (This will change in Jan. 2019)

C: Rights and Responsibilities

48. There are four amendments to the
Constitution about who can vote. Know one
of these.

 - Citizens eighteen (18) and older (can vote).
 - You don't have to pay (a poll tax) to vote.
 - Any citizen can vote. (Women and men can
   vote.)
 - A male citizen of any race (can vote).

*49. What is one responsibility that is only for
United States citizens? Both are correct.

 - to serve on a jury;
 - to vote in a federal election

50. 列舉一項美國公民才享有的權利.

- 在聯邦選舉中投票的權利
- 競選公職的權利

51. 每一個住在美國的人享有的兩項權利是什麼？

- 表達自由
- 言論自由
- 集會結社的自由
- 向政府請願的自由
- 宗教崇拜的自由
- 持有武器的自由

52. 當我們宣誓效忠時. 是向什麼表達忠誠？

- 美利堅合眾國
- 國旗

50. Name one right only for United States citizens. Both are correct.

- to vote in a federal election
- to run for federal office

51. What are <u>two</u> rights of everyone living in the United States? All are correct.

- freedom of expression
- freedom of worship
- freedom of speech
- the right to bear arms
- freedom of assembly
- freedom to petition the government

52. What do we show loyalty to when we say the Pledge of Allegiance? (Know one way to say it. Both are correct.)

- the United States
- the flag

53. 當您成為美國公民時做出的一項承諾是什麼？

- 放棄效忠其他國家
- 護衛美國的憲法及法律
- 遵守美國的法律
- (必要時) 加入美國軍隊
- (必要時) 為國效勞 (為國做重要工作)
- 效忠美國

*54. 美國公民必須幾歲才能投票選舉總統？

- 十八 (18) 歲以上

55. 美國人參與民主政治的兩種方法是什麼？

- 投票
- 加入政黨
- 協助競選活動
- 加入公民團體
- 加入社區團體
- 向民選官員提供自己對某項議題的意見
- 撥電給參議員和眾議員
- 公開支持或反對某個議題或政策
- 競選公職
- 向報社投函

53. What is <u>one</u> promise you make when you become a United States citizen?

- to give up loyalty to other countries
- to defend the Constitution and laws of the United States
- to obey the laws of the United States
- to serve in the U.S. military (if needed)
- to serve (do important work for) the nation (if needed)
- to be loyal to the United States

*54. How old do citizens have to be to vote for President?

- at least eighteen (18) years old

55. What are <u>two</u> ways that Americans can participate in their democracy? All are correct.

- vote
- join a political party
- help with a campaign
- join a civic group
- join a community group
- give an elected official your opinion on an issue
- call Senators and Representatives
- publicly support or oppose an issue or policy
- run for office write to a newspaper

*56. 寄送聯邦所得稅表的截止日期是哪一天？

- （每年的）4月15日

57. 所有男性到了哪個年齡必須註冊「兵役登記」？

- 十八 **(18)** 歲
- 十八 **(18)** 歲至二十六 **(26)** 歲之間

美國歷史

A: 殖民期與獨立

58. 殖民者當初到美國的一項理由是什麼？

- 自由
- 政治自由
- 宗教自由
- 經濟機會
- 從事宗教活動
- 逃避迫害

*56. When is the last day you can send in federal income tax forms?

   April 15

57. When must all men register for the Selective Service? (There are two ways to say it. Know one of them.)

   - at age eighteen (18)
   - between eighteen (18) and
      twenty-six (26)

The Selective Service

American History

A: Colonial Period and Independence

58. What is <u>one</u> reason colonists came to America?

   - for freedom
   - for political liberty
   - for religious freedom
   - for economic opportunity
   - to practice their religion
   - to escape persecution

59. 歐洲人抵達美國之前, 誰已經居住在美國？

- 美國印地安人
- 美國原住民

60. 哪一群人被帶到美國並被販賣為奴？

- 非洲人
- 來自非洲的人

61. 殖民者為何與英國作戰？

- 因為高額捐稅（只繳稅, 沒有代表權）
- 因為英國軍隊住在他們的住宅內（寄宿, 宿營）
- 因為他們沒有自治權

62.「獨立宣言」是誰寫的？

- （湯瑪士）傑佛遜

59. Who lived in America before the Europeans arrived? (Know one way to say it.)

 - American Indians
 - Native Americans

60. What group of people was taken to America and sold as slaves? (Know one way to say it.)

 - Africans
 - people from Africa

61. Why did the colonists fight the British? (Know one answer below)

 - because of high taxes ("taxation without representation")

 - because the British army stayed in their - houses (boarding, quartering)

 - because they didn't have self-government

62. Who wrote the Declaration of Independence? (These are two ways to say it. Both are correct.)

 - Thomas Jefferson
 - Jefferson

63. 「獨立宣言」是何時通過採用的？

   ▪ 1776 年7月4日

64. 美國原先有13個州. 請列舉其中三個州.

   ▪ 新罕布夏
   ▪ 麻薩諸塞
   ▪ 羅德島
   ▪ 康乃狄克
   ▪ 紐約
   ▪ 紐澤西
   ▪ 賓夕法尼亞
   ▪ 德拉瓦
   ▪ 馬裏蘭
   ▪ 維吉尼亞
   ▪ 北卡羅萊納
   ▪ 南卡羅萊納
   ▪ 喬治亞

65. 制憲會議達成了什麼事？

   ▪ 擬定憲法.
   ▪ 開國諸賢擬定了憲法.

63. When was the Declaration of Independence adopted?

July 4, 1776

64. There were 13 original states. Name three.

Connecticut	New York
Delaware	North Carolina
Georgia	Pennsylvania
Maryland	Rhode Island
Massachusetts	South Carolina
New Hampshire	Virginia
New Jersey	

65. What happened at the Constitutional Convention? (Know one way to say it.)

- The Constitution was written.
- The Founding Fathers wrote the Constitution.

66. 憲法是何時擬定的？

- 1787年

67. 《聯邦論》支持美國憲法的通過.
請列舉一名《聯邦論》的作者.

- （詹姆士）麥迪森
- （亞歷山大）漢米爾頓
- （約翰）傑伊
- 普布利烏斯

68 班哲明·富蘭克林著稱的一項事蹟是什麼？

- 美國外交官
- 制憲會議年紀最長的成員
- 美國第一任郵政總局局長
- 《窮人理查年鑑》的作者
- 開辦第一個免費圖書館

69. 誰是「美國國父」？

- （喬治）華盛頓

66. When was the Constitution written?

1787

67. The Federalist Papers supported the passage of the U.S. Constitution. Name <u>one</u> of the writers.

- (James) Madison
- (Alexander) Hamilton
- (John) Jay
- Publius

68. What is <u>one</u> thing Benjamin Franklin is famous for? (All are correct.)

- He was a U.S. diplomat.
- He was the oldest member of the Constitutional Convention.
- He was the first Postmaster General of the United States.
- He wrote "Poor Richard's Almanac".
- He started the first free libraries.

69. Who is the "Father of Our Country"?

(George) Washington

*70. 誰是第一任總統？

- （喬治）華盛頓

George Washington,

B: 1800 年代

71. 美國在1803年向法國購買哪塊領地？

- 路易士安納領地
- 路易士安納

72. 列舉一場美國在1800年代參與的戰爭。

- 1812年戰爭
- 美墨戰爭
- 內戰
- 美國與西班牙戰爭

*70. Who was the first President?

(George) Washington

B: The U.S. in the 1800s

71. What territory did the United States buy from France in 1803?

- the Louisiana Territory
- Louisiana

72. Name <u>one</u> war fought by the United States in the 1800s. (All are correct.)

- War of 1812
- Mexican-American War
- Civil War
- Spanish-American War

73. 請說出美國南方與北方之間戰爭的名稱．

- 內戰
- 州際戰爭

74. 列舉一項導致內戰的問題．

- 奴隸制度
- 經濟原因
- 各州的權利

*75. 亞伯拉罕・林肯的一項重要事蹟是什麼？

- 解放奴隸（《解放宣言》）
- 拯救（保留）聯盟
- 在內戰期間引領美國

Abraham Lincoln,

73. Name the U.S. war between the North and the South. (Both are correct. Most Americans call it the Civil War.)

- the Civil War
- the War between the States

74. Name <u>one</u> problem that led to the Civil War. All are correct.

- slavery
- economic reasons
- states' rights

***75. What was <u>one</u> important thing that Abraham Lincoln did? (All are correct.) He...**

- freed the slaves (with the Emancipation Proclamation)
- saved (or preserved) the Union
- led the United States during the Civil War

76.《解放宣言》達成了什麼？

- 解放了奴隸
- 解放了聯邦制下的奴隸
- 解放了聯邦各州的奴隸
- 解放了南方大部分州的奴隸

77. 蘇珊B. 安東尼的事蹟是什麼？

- 為女權奮鬥
- 為民權奮鬥

C: 美國近代史與其他重要的歷史資料

*78. 列舉一場美國在1900年代參與的戰爭. *

- 第一次世界大戰
- 第二次世界大戰
- 朝鮮戰爭
- 越戰
- (波斯灣）海灣戰爭

76. What did the Emancipation Proclamation do? (All are correct. Know one.)

-It freed the slaves.
-It freed slaves in the Confederacy,
-It freed slaves in the Confederate states,
-It freed slaves in most Southern states,

77. What did Susan B. Anthony do?

-She fought for women's rights

C: Recent American History and Other Important Historical Information

*78. Name <u>one</u> war fought by the United States in the 1900s. (All are correct.)

-World War I
-World War II
-Korean War
-Vietnam War
-(Persian) Gulf War

79. 第一次世界大戰期間的美國總統是誰？

- （伍德羅）威爾遜

80. 美國經濟大蕭條和第二次世界大戰期間的總統是誰？

- （富蘭克林）羅斯福

81. 美國在第二次世界大戰與哪些國家作戰？

- 日本、德國、義大利

82. 艾森豪在當總統以前是將軍．他曾參加哪一場戰爭？

- 第二次世界大戰

83. 在冷戰期間，美國的主要顧慮是什麼？

- 共產主義

84. 哪項運動試圖結束種族歧視？

- 民權（運動）

79. Who was President during World War I?

- (Woodrow) Wilson

80. Who was President during the Great Depression and World War II?

- (Franklin) Roosevelt

81. Who did the United States fight in World War II?

- Japan, Germany, and Italy

82. Before he was President, Eisenhower was a general. What war was he in?

-World War II

83. During the Cold War, what was the main concern of the United States?

- Communism

84. What movement tried to end racial discrimination?

-the civil rights movement

*85. 小馬丁・路德・金的事蹟是什麼？

- 為民權奮鬥
- 為所有美國人爭取平等

86. 美國在2001年9月11日發生了什麼重大事件？

- 恐怖份子攻擊美國.

87. 列舉一個美國印地安人部族.

〔USCIS主考官將有聯邦承認的美國印地安人部族清單.〕

▪賀皮	▪拉科塔
▪伊努特	▪克洛
▪切洛基	▪泰頓
▪納瓦荷	▪歐尼達
▪蘇	▪休倫
▪齊普瓦	▪莫希根
▪喬克陶	▪蕭尼
▪布耶布洛	▪阿拉瓦克
▪阿帕契	▪夏安
▪伊洛奎斯	▪賽米諾利
▪庫瑞克	▪佈雷克非特

*85. What did Martin Luther King, Jr. do? (Both are correct. Know one way to say it.)

- He fought for civil rights.
- He worked for equality for all Americans.

86. What major event happened on September 11, 2001 in the United States?

-Terrorists attacked the United States.

87. Name one American Indian tribe in the United States.

[USCIS Officers will be given a list of federally recognized American Indian tribes.]

Apache	Inuit
Arawak	Iroquois
Blackfeet	Lakota
Cherokee	Mohegan
Cheyenne	Navajo
Chippewa	Oneida
Choctaw	Pueblo
Creek	Seminole
Crow	Shawnee
Hopi	Sioux
Huron	Teton

A: 地理

88. 列舉美國最長的兩條河中的一條．

   ▪ 密蘇裏（河）
   ▪ 密西西比（河）

89. 美國西岸瀕臨什麼海洋？

   ▪ 太平洋

90. 美國東岸瀕臨什麼海洋？

   ▪ 大西洋

91. 列舉一個美國領地．

   ▪ 波多黎各
   ▪ 美屬維京群島
   ▪ 美屬薩摩亞
   ▪ 北馬裏亞納群島
   ▪ 關島

Integrated Civics

A: Geography

88. Name <u>one</u> of the two longest rivers in the United States.

  - the Mississippi (River)
  - the Missouri (River)

89. What ocean is on the West Coast of the United States?

  - the Pacific (Ocean)

90. What ocean is on the East Coast of the United States?

  - the Atlantic (Ocean)

91. Name <u>one</u> U.S. territory.

  - Puerto Rico
  - U.S. Virgin Islands
  - American Samoa
  - Northern Mariana Islands
  - Guam

92. 列舉一個與加拿大毗連的州.

- 緬因　　　　　　· 明尼蘇達
- 新罕布夏　　　　· 北達科他
- 佛蒙特　　　　　· 蒙大拿
- 紐約　　　　　　· 愛達荷
- 賓夕法尼亞　　　· 華盛頓
- 俄亥俄　　　　　· 阿拉斯加
- 密西根

93. 列舉一個與墨西哥毗連的州.

- 加利福尼亞
- 亞利桑那
- 新墨西哥
- 德克薩斯

*94. 美國的首都在哪裡？

- 華盛頓哥倫比亞特區

*95. 自由女神像在哪裡？

- 紐約（港）
- 自由島

〔回答紐澤西、紐約市附近、哈德遜河上也可以接受〕

92. Name <u>one</u> state that borders Canada.

Alaska	New York
Idaho	North Dakota
Maine	Ohio
Michigan	Pennsylvania
Minnesota	Vermont
Montana	Washington
New Hampshire	

93. Name <u>one</u> state that borders Mexico.

- California
- Arizona
- New Mexico
- Texas

*94. What is the capital of the United States?

Washington, D.C.

*95. Where is the Statue of Liberty? (These both mean the same place. Know <u>one</u> of these. All are correct.)

- New York Harbor
- Liberty Island

[Also acceptable are "New Jersey", "near New York City", or "on the Hudson (River)".]

B: 標誌

96. 國旗上為什麼有十三個條紋？

- 因為當初有十三個殖民地
- 因為條紋代表當初的殖民地

*97. 國旗上為什麼有五十顆星星？

- 因為一個州有一顆星
- 因為一顆星代表一個州
- 因為有五十個州

98. 美國國歌的名稱是什麼？

- 星條旗之歌

C: 國定假日

*99. 我們在哪一天慶祝獨立紀念日？

- 7月4日

B: Symbols

96. Why does the flag have 13 stripes? (Know one way to say it.)

- because there were 13 original colonies
- because the stripes represent the original colonies

*97. Why does the flag have 50 stars?

- because each star represents a state and there are 50 states.
- because there is one star for each state
- because there are 50 states

98. What is the name of the national anthem?

- The Star-Spangled Banner

C: Holidays

*99. When do we celebrate Independence Day?

- July 4th (July Fourth)

The Statue of Liberty

100. 列舉<u>兩個</u>美國的國定假日：

- 新年

- 馬丁路德金的生日

- 總統日

- 國殤日

- 美國國慶日

- 勞動節

- 哥倫布日

- 退伍軍人節

- 感恩節

- 聖誕節

美國國慶日

100. Name two national U.S. holidays.

    -New Year's Day

    -Martin Luther King, Jr. Day

    -Presidents' Day

    -Memorial Day

    -Independence Day

    -Labor Day

    -Columbus Day

    -Veterans Day

    -Thanksgiving

    -Christmas

65/20

如果您已年滿65歲或65歲以上，並且已經持有美國合法永久居留權(俗稱綠卡)20年或更久，則您只需要研讀標示有星號的考題。

The 20 Civics Questions
for People 65 and older

65/20
(USCIS)

*If you are 65 years old or older and have been a legal permanent resident of the United States for 20 or more years, you only need to know the questions that have been marked with an asterisk.(*) They are also listed below.

The 20 questions for qualified permanent residents over 65 are: #6, 11, 13, 17, 20, 27, 28, 44, 45, 49, 54, 56, 70, 75, 78, 85, 94, 95, 97, 99

65/20
(USCIS)

如果您已年滿65歲或65歲以上,
並且已經持有美國合法永久居留權 (俗稱綠卡) 20年或更久,
您只需要研讀標示有星號 (*) 的考題.

#6, 11, 13, 17, 20, 27, 28, 44, 45, 49, 54, 56, 70, 75, 78, 85, 94, 95, 97, 99

如果您年齡在65歲以上，並且在美國有合法永久居留權20年以上，您只需要研究這些問題（*）.

A: 美國民主原則

*6. 列舉憲法第一條修正案中的一項權利或自由？

- 言論自由
- 宗教自由
- 集會結社的自由
- 出版自由
- 向政府請願的自由

*11. 美國的經濟制度是什麼？

- 資本主義經濟
- 市場經濟

B: 政治體制

*13. 列舉政府體制的一個分支或部門.

- 立法部門 (國會)
- 行政部門 (總統)
- 司法部門 (法院)

65/20

20 Civics Questions
for People 65 and older

A. Principles of American Democracy

*6. What is <u>one</u> right or freedom from the First Amendment? All are correct.

- speech
- religion
- assembly
- press
- petition the government

*11. What is the economic system in the United States? (Know one way to say it. Both are correct.)

- capitalist economy
- market economy

B: U.S. System of Government

*13. Name one branch or part of the government.

- the legislative branch (the Congress)
- the executive branch (the president)
- the judicial branch (the courts)

*17. 美國國會由哪兩個部分組成？

  ▪ 參議院與眾議院

*20.您所在州的現任一位美國參議員的名字是什麼？

  ▪ 答案依所在州不同而異
 .〔住在哥倫比亞特區和美國領
   土的居民可答:哥倫比亞特區當地
   （或應試居民所在領地） 沒有美國參議員.〕

*27. 我們在哪一個月選總統？

  ▪ 十一月

*28. 現任美國總統的名字是什麼？

  ▪ Donald Trump
  ▪ Trump

President Donald Trump

*17. What are the <u>two</u> parts of the U.S Congress?

> -the Senate and the House (of Representatives)

*20. Who is one of your state's U.S. senators now?

My senator is: _____

Answers will be different for each state. [District of Columbia residents and residents of U.S. territories should answer that D.C. (or the territory where the applicant lives) has no U.S. Senators.] If you don't know the answer, ask your local librarian. Or go to this website:

www.senate.gov

*27. In what month do we vote for President?

> - November

*28. What is the name of the President of the United States now?

> - Donald Trump
> - Trump

*44. 您居住州的首府是哪裡？

▪ 答案依居住州不同而異.〔哥倫比亞特區居民應回答哥
倫比亞特區不是一個州, 沒有首府. 美國領地居民應回答
居住領地的首府.〕

Alabama - Montgomery

Alaska - Juneau

Arizona - Phoenix

Arkansas - Little Rock

California -Sacramento

Colorado - Denver

Connecticut -Hartford

Delaware - Dover

Florida - Tallahassee

Georgia - Atlanta

Hawaii - Honolulu

Idaho - Boise

Illinois - Springfield

Indiana - Indianapolis

Iowa - Des Moines

Kansas - Topeka

Kentucky - Frankfort

Louisiana - Baton Rouge

Maine - Augusta

Maryland - Annapolis

Massachusetts - Boston

Michigan - Lansing

Minnesota - St. Paul

Mississippi - Jackson

Missouri - Jefferson City

Montana - Helena

Nebraska - Lincoln

Nevada - Carson City

New Hampshire - Concord

New Jersey - Trenton

New Mexico - Santa Fe

New York - Albany

North Carolina – Raleigh

North Dakota - Bismarck

Ohio - Columbus

Oklahoma - Oklahoma City

Oregon - Salem

Pennsylvania - Harrisburg

Rhode Island - Providence

South Carolina - Columbia

South Dakota - Pierre

Tennessee - Nashville

Texas - Austin

Utah - Salt Lake City

Vermont - Montpelier

Virginia - Richmond

Washington - Olympia

West Virginia - Charleston

Wisconsin - Madison

Wyoming - Cheyenne

*44. What is the capital of your state?

Answers will be different by state. [People who live in the District of Columbia should answer that D.C. is not a state and does not have a capital. Residents of U.S. territories should name the capital of the territory.]

Alabama - Montgomery

Alaska - Juneau

Arizona - Phoenix

Arkansas - Little Rock

California -Sacramento

Colorado - Denver

Connecticut -Hartford

Delaware - Dover

Florida - Tallahassee

Georgia - Atlanta

Hawaii - Honolulu

Idaho - Boise

Illinois - Springfield

Indiana - Indianapolis

Iowa - Des Moines

Kansas - Topeka

Kentucky - Frankfort

Louisiana - Baton Rouge

Maine - Augusta

Maryland - Annapolis

Massachusetts - Boston

Michigan - Lansing

Minnesota - St. Paul

Mississippi - Jackson

Missouri - Jefferson City

Montana - Helena

Nebraska - Lincoln

Nevada - Carson City

New Hampshire - Concord

New Jersey - Trenton

New Mexico - Santa Fe

New York - Albany

North Carolina – Raleigh

North Dakota - Bismarck

Ohio - Columbus

Oklahoma - Oklahoma City

Oregon - Salem

Pennsylvania - Harrisburg

Rhode Island - Providence

South Carolina - Columbia

South Dakota - Pierre

Tennessee - Nashville

Texas - Austin

Utah - Salt Lake City

Vermont - Montpelier

Virginia - Richmond

Washington - Olympia

West Virginia - Charleston

Wisconsin - Madison

Wyoming – Cheyenne

*45. 美國當今兩大政黨為何？

- 民主黨與共和黨

C: 權利與責任

*49. 列舉一項美國公民才有的責任？

- 當陪審員
- 在聯邦選舉中投票

*54. 美國公民必須幾歲才能投票選舉總統？

- 十八 **(18)** 歲以上

*56. 寄送聯邦所得稅表的截止日期是哪一天？

- （每年的）**4**月**15**日

美國歷史

A: 殖民期與獨立

*70. 誰是第一任總統？

- （喬治）華盛頓

*45. What are the two major political parties in the United States?

- Democratic and Republican

C. Rights and Responsibilities of Citizens

*49. What is one responsibility that is only for United States citizens? (Know one for the test. Both are correct.)

- serve on a jury
- vote in a federal election

*54. How old do citizens have to be to vote for President?

- eighteen (18) and older

*56. When is the last day you can send in federal income tax forms?

- April 15

American History

A. Colonial Period and Independence

*70. Who was the first President?

- (George) Washington

B: 1800 年代

*75. 亞伯拉罕‧林肯的一項重要事蹟是什麼？

- 解放奴隸（《解放宣言》）
- 拯救（保留）聯盟
- 在內戰期間引領美國

C: 美國近代史與其他重要的歷史資料

*78. 列舉一場美國在1900年代參與的戰爭.

- 第一次世界大戰
- 第二次世界大戰
- 朝鮮戰爭
- 越戰
- 波斯灣）海灣戰爭

*85. 小馬丁‧路德‧金的事蹟是什麼？

- 為民權奮鬥
- 為所有美國人爭取平等

B. The U.S. in the 1980s

*75. What was <u>one</u> important thing that Abraham Lincoln did? (All are correct.)

- He freed the slaves (with the Emancipation Proclamation).
- He saved (or preserved) the Union.
- He led the United States during the Civil War.

C. Recent American History and Other Important Historical Information

*78. Name <u>one</u> war fought by the United States in the 1900s. (All are correct.)

- World War I
- World War II
- Korean War
- Vietnam War
- (Persian) Gulf War

*85. What did Martin Luther King, Jr. do?

- He fought for civil rights.
- He worked for equality for all Americans.

A: 地理

*94. 美國的首都在哪裡？

　　▪華盛頓哥倫比亞特區

*95. 自由女神像在哪裡？

　　▪紐約（港）
　　▪自由島
〔回答紐澤西、紐約市附近、哈德遜河上也可以接受〕

B: 標誌

*97. 國旗上為什麼有五十顆星星？

　　▪因為一個州有一顆星
　　▪因為一顆星代表一個州
　　▪因為有五十個州

C: 國定假日

*99. 我們在哪一天慶祝獨立紀念日？

　　▪7月4日

Integrated Civics

A. Geography

*94. What is the capital of the United States?

- Washington, D.C.

*95. Where is the Statue of Liberty?
(Know one way to say it. Both are correct.)

- New York Harbor
- Liberty Island

B. Symbols

*97. Why does the flag have 50 stars?

- because each star represents one state and there are 50 states.

C. Holidays

*99. When do we celebrate Independence Day?

-July 4

II

English

Practice Civics Quiz: Multiple Choice

At your naturalization interview, you will be asked 6-10 questions from the list of 100 civics questions in the previous section. You will need to tell the interviewer your answers orally. You will **not** be given a multiple choice test.

But the multiple choice quiz in the next section gives you another helpful way to practice for the USCIS oral civics test. These questions are the same ones asked in Part I, but they are asked in a different way to give you a different kind of practice.

The answers are at the bottom of each page, for easy review. They follow the same order as the USCIS questions that begin on page 15.

Practice Civics Quiz – Multiple Choice

1. What is the "supreme law of the land"?

a. the Supreme Court
b. the President
c. the Declaration of Independence
d. the Constitution

2. What does the Constitution do?

a. sets up the government
b. explains the Declaration of Independence
c. limits immigration
d. describes the nation's freedom from England

3. The idea of self-government is in the first three words of the Constitution. What are these words?

a. Congress shall make
b. We the People
c. We, the colonists
d. All men are created equal

4. What is an amendment?

a. the beginning of the Declaration of Independence
b. the Preamble to the Constitution
c. a change or addition to the Constitution
d. an introduction

5. What do we call the first ten amendments to the Constitution?

a. the Declaration of Independence
b. the Bill of Rights
c. the inalienable rights
d. the Articles of Confederation

Answers: 1 – d, 2 - a, 3 - b, 4 - c, 5 – b

*6. What is one right or freedom in the First Amendment?

a. the right to bear arms
b. the right to vote
c. the right to free speech
d. the right to trial by jury

7. How many amendments does the Constitution have?

a. 10
b. 15
c. 22
d. 27

8. What did the Declaration of Independence say?

a. that all Americans are independent from the government
b. that the British colonists in North America were creating their own independent country
c that colonial America was independent from Canada
d. that American was independent from France

9. What are two rights in the Declaration of Independence?

a. the right to happiness and a good job
b. liberty and an independent government
c. liberty and the pursuit of happiness
d. wealth and good health

10. What is freedom of religion?

a. You must choose a religion.
b. You can have any religion you want or not have a religion.
c. You can choose the time you observe your religion.
d. You do not need to pay to join a church or temple.

Answers: 6 - c, 7 - d, 8 - b, 9 - c, 10 - b

*11. What is the economic system of the United States?

a. socialism
b. capitalism
c. democracy
d. communism

12. What is the rule of law?

a. Everyone must follow the law.
b. Everyone but the President must follow the law.
c. The president makes the laws.
d. All laws must be the same in every state.

*13. Name one branch of government.

a. the Supreme Court
b. state government
c. the House of Representatives
d. the executive

14. What stops any one branch of government from becoming too powerful?

a. the power of the presidency
b. the voters
c. checks and balances
d. freedom of speech

15. Who is in charge of the executive branch?

a. the President
b. the Secretary of Defense
c. the Vice President
d. the Congress

Answers: 11 – b, 12 – a, 13 – d, 14 – c, 15 – a

16. Who makes federal laws?

a. the Supreme Court
b. the President
c. Congress
d. the states

*17. What are the two parts to the U.S. Congress?

a. the Supreme Court and the lower courts
b. the Senate and all the state governors
c. the House of Lords and the House of Commons
d. the Senate and House of Representatives

18. How many U.S. senators are there in the Senate?

a. 50
b. 2
c. 100
d. 200

19. How many years is a senator elected for each term?

a. ten (10)
b. six (6)
c. four (4)
d. two (2)

*20. Who is one of your state's U.S. senators?

_____

Answers: 16 - c, 17 - d, 18 - c, 19 - b, 20 - your answer —
check **www.usa.gov** or ask a librarian

21. How many voting members does the House of Representatives have?

a. 100
b. 200
c. 435
d. 365

22. We elect a U.S. Representative for how many years?

a. eight (8)
b. four (4)
c. two (2)
d. six (6)

23. Name your representative.

_____

24. Who does a U.S. Senator represent?

a. the state legislatures
b. all the people of his state
c. only the people in the state who voted for the senator
d. all the people of the state who belong to the senator's political party

25. Why do some states have more representatives than others?

a. larger states get more representatives.
b. the number of representatives is based on the population in the state.
c. states that have been part of the U.S. longer have more representatives.
d. small states do not have many representatives.

Answers: 21 - c; 22 - c; 23 - your representative: check *www.usa.gov* or call your local library; 24 - b, 25 - b

26. How many years does a President serve in one term?

a. eight (8)
b. two (2)
c. six (6)
d. four (4)

*27. In what month do we elect a president?

a. July
b. November
c. January
d. October

*28. Who is President of the United States now?

a. Mike Pence
b. Barack Obama
c. Donald Trump
d. Franklin Roosevelt

29. Who is Vice President now?

a. Mike Pence
b. Hillary Clinton
c. Barack Obama
d. Thomas Jefferson

30. If the President can no longer serve, who becomes President?

a. the President Pro-Tempore
b. the Secretary of State
c. the Vice President
d. the President

Answers: 26 - d, 27 - b, 28 - c, 29 - a, 30 - c

31. If the President and Vice President can no longer serve, who becomes President?

a. the Speaker of the House
b. the Secretary of State
c. the Vice President
d. the Secretary of Defense

32. Who is the Commander-in-Chief of the military?

a. the Vice President
b. the President
c. General Pershing
d. the Secretary of Defense

33. Who signs the bills from Congress to make them into laws?

a. the President of the Senate
b. the vice President
c. the Speaker of the House
d. the President

34. Who can veto bills from Congress?

a. the Vice President
b. the President
c. the Speaker of the House
d. the President Pro Tempore

35. What does the President's Cabinet do?

a. writes the yearly budget to submit to Congress
b. approves presidential appointments
c. advises the President
d. works closely with Congress

Answers: 31 - a, 32 - b, 33 - d, 34 - b, 35 - c

36. Which of the following are two Cabinet-level positions?

a. Secretary of State and Secretary of the Treasury
b. Secretary of Health and Human Services and Secretary of the Navy
c. Secretary of Weather and Secretary of Energy
d. Secretary of the Interior and Secretary of History

37. What does the judicial branch of government do?

a. reviews and explains laws
b. appoints judges
c. makes laws
d. chooses Supreme Court judges

38. What is the highest court in the country?

a. the Appeals Court
b. the Supreme Court
c. superior courts
d. district courts

39. How many justices are on the Supreme Court?

a. eleven (11)
b. ten (10)
c. nine (9)
d. twelve (12)

40 . Who is the Chief Justice of the United States now?

a. Barack Obama
b. Donald Trump
c. Anthony Kennedy
d. John Roberts

Answers: 36 - a, 37 - a, 38 - b, 39 - c, 40 - d

41. Under our Constitution, some powers belong to the federal government. What is one power of the federal government?

a. to make treaties with foreign governments
b. to set up police departments
c. to build all schools
d. to issue driver's licenses

42. The Constitution gives powers to the states. Which of the following is not a state power?

a to issue driver's licenses
b. to collect taxes
c. to print money
d. to provide safety for the public (police and fire departments)

43. Who is the governor of your state?

_____

*44. What is your state capital?

_____

*45. What are the two major political parties in the United States today?

a. American and Bull-Moose
b. Democratic and Republican
c. Democratic-Republican and Whigs
d. Libertarian and Green

Answers; 41 - a, 42 - c, 43 - check **www.usa.gov** for your state's governor; 44 - see p.35; 45 - b

46. What is the political party of the President now?

a. Democratic Party
b. Independent Party
c. Green Party
d. Republican Party

47. What is the name of the current Speaker of the House? (This is correct until January 2019. Then go to: www.lakewoodpublishing.com or www.uscis.gov.)

a. Barack Obama
b. Donald Trump
c. Paul Ryan
d. Mitch McConnell

48. There are four amendments to the Constitution about voting. Describe one of them.

a. Only citizens by birth can vote.
b. Only citizens older than 21 can vote.
c. Citizens eighteen (18) and older can vote.
d. Only citizens with a job can vote.

*49. Which of the following is not a responsibility for all U.S. citizens?

a. serve on a jury
b. get a passport
c. vote
d. pay taxes

50. Which of the following rights is only for U.S. citizens?

a. to pay taxes
b. to go to college
c. to get medical care
d. to vote

Answers: 46 - d, 47 - c, 48 - c, 49 - b, 50 - d

51. Which two rights are for citizens and non-citizens living in the U.S.?

a. freedom of speech and the right to vote
b. freedom of speech and serving on a jury
c. freedom of speech and freedom of religion
d. the right to vote and the right to travel with a U.S. passport

52. What do we show loyalty to when we say the Pledge of Allegiance?

a. the Founding Fathers
b. the United States
c. the Constitution
d. the U.S. military

53. What is one promise that you make when you become a U.S. citizen?

a. to bring your family to the United States
b. to get a driver's license
c. to be loyal to the United States
d. to get an American passport

*54. How old are U.S. citizens when they can begin to vote?

a. 21
b. 18
c. 25
d. 20

55. What are two ways that Americans can participate in their democracy?

a. vote and join a civic group
b. give an elected official your opinion on an issue and vote
c. write to a newspaper and call their congressmen
d. all of these answers

Answers: 51 - c, 52 - b, 53 - c, 54 - b, 55 - d

*56. When is the last day you can send in federal income tax forms?

a. July 4
b. April 15
c. May 15
d. March 15

57. When must all men register for the Selective Service?

a. between eighteen (18) and twenty-six (26)
b. at any age
c. only at age eighteen (18)
d. American men do not have to register

58. Why did colonists come to America?

a. for religious freedom
b. for political freedom
c. for economic opportunities
d. all of the above

59. Who lived in America before the Europeans arrived?

a. no one
b. Floridians
c. American Indians
d. Canadians

60. What group of people was captured and taken to America then sold as slaves?

a. English settlers
b. Canadians
c. Dutch
d. Africans

Answers: 56 - b, 57 - a, 58 - d, 59 - c, 60 - d

61. Why did the colonists fight the British?

a. because they didn't have self-government
b. because of unfair taxes
c. because the British army stayed in the colonists homes
d. all of these answers

62. Who wrote the Declaration of Independence?

a. George Washington
b. Thomas Jefferson
c. Benjamin Franklin
d. James Madison

63. When was the Declaration of Independence adopted?

a. July 4, 1776
b. January 1, 1775
c. December 10, 1776
d. July 1, 1775

64. There were 13 original states. Which of the following were included?

a. Georgia, Maine, Texas
b. New Hampshire, New York, New Mexico
c. Georgia, Pennsylvania, New York
d. Rhode Island, Delaware, Washington

65. What happened at the Constitutional Convention?

a. The Constitution was presented to King George
b. The Constitution was written
c. They wrote the Bill of Rights
d. They wrote the Declaration of Independence

Answers: 61 - d, 62 - b, 63 - a, 64 - c, 65 - b

66. When was the Constitution written?

a. 1776
b. 1787
c. 1789
d. 1790

67. The Federalist Papers supported the passage of the U.S. Constitution. Name one writer.

a. John Adams
b. George Washington
c. James Madison
d. Thomas Jefferson

68. What is one thing Benjamin Franklin is famous for?

a. He was the youngest member of the Constitutional
   Convention.
b. He was third President of the United States.
c. He was a writer and diplomat.
d. all of the above

69. Who is "The Father of Our Country"?

a. George Washington
b. Barack Obama
c. John F. Kennedy
d. Abraham Lincoln

*70. Who was the first president of the United States?

a. Thomas Jefferson
b. George Washington
c. James Madison
d. John Adams

Answers: 66 - b, 67 - c, 68 - c, 69 - a, 70 - b

71. What territory did the United States buy from France in 1803?

a. Quebec
b. Haiti
c. Louisiana
d. Alaska

72. Name one war fought by the U.S. in the 1800s (the nineteenth century).

a. World War II
b. Civil War
c. Korean War
d. World War I

73. Name the U.S. war between the northern and southern states.

a. the American Revolution
b. the Civil War
c. the War of 1812
d. the Vietnam War

74. Which of these problems led to the Civil War?

a. slavery
b. economic conflicts
c. international treaties
d. a and b

*75. What was one important thing that Abraham Lincoln did?

a. established the United Nations
b. lead the U.S. to victory in World War I
c. saved (or preserved) the Union
d. purchased Alaska for the United States

Answers: 71 - c, 72 - b, 73 - b, 74 - d, 75 - c

76. What did the Emancipation Proclamation do?

a. freed the slaves
b. gave women the right to vote
c. ended the Civl War
d. ended World War I

77. Which of the following women fought for women's right to vote?

a. Emily Dickinson
b. Martha Washington
c. Susan B. Anthony
d. Dolley Madison

*78. Name one war fought by the U.S. in the 1900s (the twentieth century).

a. the French-Indian War
b. the Korean War
c. the Spanish-American War
d. the Mexican-American War

79. Who was President during World War I?

a. Theodore Roosevelt
b. Franklin Roosevelt
c. Woodrow Wilson
d. Warren Harding

80. Who was President during World War II?

a. Theodore Roosevelt
b. Franklin Roosevelt
c. Woodrow Wilson
d. Warren Harding

Answers: 76 - a, 77 - c, 78 - b, 79 - c, 80 - b

81. Who did the U.S. fight in WWII?

a. Japan
b. Germany
c. Italy
d. all of the above

82. Before he was President, Eisenhower was a general. Which war was he in?

a. Civil War
b. World War II
c. Spanish-American War
d. Vietnam War

83. During the Cold War, what was the main concern of the United States?

a. the Great Depression
b. climate change
c. communism
d. slavery

84. What movement tried to end racial discrimination?

a. civil rights movement
b. conservation
c. prohibition
d. women's suffrage

*85. What did Dr. Martin Luther King, Jr. do?

a. wrote the Declaration of Independence
b. ended slavery
c. led peaceful protests for civil rights
d. was the first African-American Secretary of State

Answers: 81 - d, 82 - b, 83 - c, 84 - a, 85 - c

86. What major event happened on September 11, 2001 in the United States?

a. Hurricane Andrew struck the southern United States
b. There was a nuclear accident at Three-Mile Island
c. Terrorists attacked the United States
d. The Japanese attacked Pearl Harbor

87. Which of the following is not an American Indian (Native American) tribe?

a. Cherokee
b. Celts
c. Crow
d. Apache

88. Which of the following is the longest river in the United States?

a. the Columbia River
b. the Missouri River
c. the Colorado River
d. the Hudson River

89. Which ocean is on the West Coast of the United States?

a. Pacific Ocean
b. Arctic Ocean
c. Indian Ocean
d. Atlantic Ocean

90. What ocean is on the East Coast of the United States?

a. Pacific Ocean
b. Arctic Ocean
c. Indian Ocean
d. Atlantic Ocean

Answers: 86 - c, 87 - b, 88 - b, 89 - a, 90 - d

91. Which of the following is not a U.S. territory?

a. American Samoa
b. Okinawa
c. Puerto Rico
d. Guam

92. Name one state that borders Canada.

a. Rhode Island
b. South Dakota
c. Maine
d. Oregon

93. Which state borders Mexico?

a. Kansas
b. Texas
c. Utah
d. Washington

*94. What is the capitol city of the U.S.?

a. New York City, NY.
b. Washington, D.C.
c. Hollywood, California
d. Boston, Massachusetts

*95. Where is the Statue of Liberty?

a. Long Island
b. New York Harbor
c. San Francisco Bay
d. Boston Harbor

Answers: 91 - b, 92 - c, 93 - b, 94 - b, 95 - b

96. Why does the flag have 13 stripes?

a. because the stripes represent the 13 members of the `` Second Continental Congress
b. because it was good luck to have 13 stripes on a flag
c. because the stripes represent the original 13 colonies
d. because there were 13 signatures on the Declaration of Independence

*97. Why does the flag have 50 stars?

a. for the 50 original Founding Fathers of America
b. for the 50 states
c. for the original 50 colonies
d. for the 50 departments in the federal government

98. What is the U.S. national anthem?

a. "Stars and Stripes Forever"
b. "America, the Beautiful"
c. "The Star-Spangled Banner"
d. "Grand Old Flag"

*99. When do we celebrate Independence Day?

a. July 4
b. January 1
c. October 31
d. April 15

100. Which of the following are not two official national holidays?

a. Christmas and Thanksgiving
b. Presidents' Day and Columbus Day
c. Veteran's Day and Memorial Day
d. Valentine's Day and Halloween

Answers: 96 - c, 97 - b, 98 - c, 99 - a, 100 - d

Reading Vocabulary - USCIS

Reading Vocabulary (USCIS List)

At your naturalization interview, the USCIS officer will show you 1-3 sentences in English. You must read one (1) of these three (3) sentences correctly to show that you can read English. The following list shows the words that USCIS recommends that you should know. You will not know the sentences that USCIS will ask you to read until you take the test.

Question Words

how
what
when
where
why
who
the
to
we

Other

a
for
here
in
of
on

Verbs

can
come
do/does
elects
have/has
be/is/are/was
lives/lived

Other

colors
dollar bill
first
largest
many
most
north

Verbs

meet
name
pay
vote
want

Other

one
people
second
south

People

George Washington
Abraham Lincoln

Places

America
United States
U.S.

Civics

American flag
Bill of Rights
capital
citizen
city
Congress
country
Father of Our Country
government
President
right
Senators
state/states
White House

Holidays

Presidents' Day
Memorial Day
Flag Day
Independence Day
Labor Day
Columbus Day
Thanksgiving

Writing Vocabulary - USCIS

Writing Vocabulary (USCIS List)

The following list shows the words that USCIS recommends that you know for the writing test. The USCIS officer will read 1-3 sentences to you. You must write one (1) of these three (3) sentences correctly to show that you can write in English. You will not know the sentences that USCIS will ask you to write until the day of the test.

Civics

American Indian
capital
citizens
Civil War
Congress
Father of Our Country
flag
free
freedom of speech
President
right
senators
state/states
White House

Months

February
May
June
July
September
October
November

People

Washington
Adams
Lincoln

Holidays

Presidents' Day
Columbus Day
Thanksgiving
Flag Day

Labor Day
Memorial Day
Independence Day

Places

Alaska
California
Canada
Delaware
Mexico
New York City
Washington, D.C.
United States

Verbs

be/is/was
can
come
elect
have/has
lives/lived
meets
pay
vote
want

Other

blue
dollar bill
fifty / 50
first
largest
most
north
one

Other

one hundred/ 100
people
red
second
south
taxes
white

Other

and
during
for
here
in

of
on
the
to
we

You can use the space below to practice writing difficult words separately or to make your own practice sentences.

★Remember: Every sentence begins with a capital letter. Every sentence ends with a period. Every question ends with a question mark.

★Remember: Capitalize words correctly. The first letter in a sentence is always capitalized. So are names of people. Pay attention to the places and things that are capitalized in the USCIS lists above.

★**An example of a sentence is below. Be sure to begin with a capital letter and end with a period.**

George Washington was the first president of the United States of America.

★**An example of a question is below. Be sure to begin with a capital letter and end with a question mark.**

What are the colors of the American flag?

Use the lines below to practice writing any difficult writing vocabulary and combining words in sentences.

_____

_____

_____

_____

_____

For More Information
Helpful U.S. Government Addresses, Websites, and Phone Numbers

For More Information
Helpful U.S. Government Addresses,
Websites, and Phone Numbers

FEDERAL DEPARTMENTS AND AGENCIES

If you don't know where to begin, call: 1-800-FED-INFO (or 1-800-333-4636) for more information. If you are hard-of-hearing, call 1-800-326-2996. The government also has a citizenship website: **http://www.USA.gov**. Look there for general information about government agencies. For forms and other citizenship information, you can also go to the USCIS website at: **www.uscis.gov**. A U.S. government website will end in ".gov".

Department of Education (ED)

U.S. Department of Education
400 Maryland Avenue SW
Washington, DC 20202
Phone: 1-800-872-5327
For hearing impaired: 1-800-437-0833
http://www.ed.gov

Department of Health and Human Services (HHS)

U.S. Department of Health and Human Services
200 Independence Avenue SW
Washington, DC 20201
Phone: 1-877-696-6775
http://www.hhs.gov

Department of Homeland Security (DHS)

U.S. Department of Homeland Security
Washington, DC 20528
http://www.dhs.gov

121

Department of Housing and Urban Development (HUD)

U.S. Department of Housing and Urban Development
451 7th Street SW
Washington, DC 20410
Phone: 202-708-1112
For hearing impaired: 202-708-1455
http://www.hud.gov

Department of Justice (DOJ)

U.S. Department of Justice
950 Pennsylvania Avenue NW
Washington, DC 20530-0001
Phone: 202-514-2000
http://www.usdoj.gov

Department of State (DOS)

U.S. Department of State
2201 C Street NW
Washington, DC 20520
Phone: 202-647-4000
http://www.state.gov

Equal Employment Opportunity Commission (EEOC)

U.S. Equal Employment Opportunity Commission
1801 L Street NW
Washington, DC 20507
Phone: 1-800-669-4000
For hearing impaired: 1-800-669-6820
http://www.eeoc.gov

Internal Revenue Service (IRS)

Phone: 1-800-829-1040
For hearing impaired: 1-800-829-4059
http://www.irs.gov

Selective Service System (SSS)

Registration Information Office
PO Box 94638
Palatine, IL 60094-4638
Phone: 847-688-6888
http://www.sss.gov

Social Security Administration (SSA)

Office of Public Inquiries
6401 Security Boulevard
Baltimore, MD 21235
Phone: 1-800-772-1213
For hearing impaired: 1-800-325-0778
http://www.socialsecurity.gov or
http://www.segurosocial.gov/espanol/.

U.S. Citizenship and Immigration Services (USCIS)

Phone: 1-800-375-5283
For hearing impaired: 1-800-767-1833
http://www.uscis.gov

U.S. Customs and Border Protection (CBP)

Phone: 202-354-1000
http://www.cbp.gov

U.S. Immigration and Customs Enforcement (ICE)

http://www.ice.gov

Flashcards

100 Civics Questions
Flashcard Format

Directions:

You can make your own flashcards by cutting the paper in this section as directed. (The questions are on the front. The answers are on the back). Then use them to study, practice and review the civics questions.

1. Remove the next pages from this book. Tear and trim or you can remove them with an exacto knife.

2. Cut each page on the dotted lines ✂--------
so that you have four separate questions/answers from each page.

3. You can keep these flashcards in an envelope.

4. Practice. Read the question on the front and give the answer. Then look at the back to see if your answer was correct.

front

	back	
What is the supreme law of the land?		The Constitution

5. Keep the questions that you miss in a separate group from the questions that you already know the answers to. Practice the ones you don't know again and again.

1. What is the supreme (highest) law of the land?

2. What does the Constitution do?

3. The idea of self-government is in the first three words of the Constitution. What are these words?

4. What is an amendment?

1. the Constitution

2. It sets up the government

   You need to know one answer.
   For more choices, see page 15.

3. We the People

4. a change to the Constitution

5. What do we call the first ten amendments to the Constitution?

----

*6. What is one right or freedom in the First Amendment?

----

7. How many amendments does the Constitution have?

----

8. What did the Declaration of Independence do?

5. the Bill of Rights

*6. freedom of religion

   You need to know one answer for USCIS.
   For other correct answers, see page 17.

7. Twenty-seven (27)

8. It announced our independence
   (from Great Britain).

   You need to know one answer.
   For more choices, see page 17.

9. What are two rights in the
   Declaration of Independence?

----

10. What is freedom of religion?

----

*11. What is the economic system in the
     United States?

----

12. What is the "rule of law"?

9. -life
   -liberty

   You need to know two rights.
   For more choices, see page 17.

10. People can observe (have) any
    religion or no religion

*11. capitalist economy

12. Everyone must follow the law.

    You need to know one answer.
    For other choices, see page 19.

*13. Name one branch or part of
the government.

- -

14. What stops one branch of
government from becoming too
powerful?

- -

15. Who is in charge of the
executive branch?

- -

16. Who makes federal laws?

*13. the legislative branch. (Congress)

You need to know one branch.
For other choices, see page 19.

14. checks and balances

15. the President

16. Congress

* 17. What are the two parts of
       the U.S. Congress?

----

18. How many U.S. senators
     are there in the Senate?

----

19. We elect a U.S. senator for
     how many years per term?

----

*20. Who is one of your state's
      U.S. senators now?

*17. the Senate and House of
    Representatives

18. one hundred (100)

19. six (6)

*20. Answers will differ. If you don't know who
    your senator is, go online to www.senate.gov.

    [Residents of the District of Columbia or
    U.S .territories should say that they have no
    U.S. senators.]

21. The House of Representatives has how many voting members?

----

22. We elect a U.S. representative for how many years per term?

----

23. Name your U.S. representative.

----

24. Who does a U.S. senator represent?

21. four hundred thirty-five (435)

22. two (2)

23. Answers will depend on where you live.
    If you don't know who your representative is,
    go online to www.usa.gov.

[If you live in a territory, not a state, you can say
that "the territory has no voting representatives in
Congress."]

24. All the people of his or her state.

25. Why do some states have more
    representatives than other states?

----

26. We elect a President for how many
    years per term?

----

*27. In what month do we vote
     for President?

----

*28. What is the name of the President of
     the United States now?

25. Because they have more people in their state.

You need to know one correct answer.
For other choices, see page 25.

26. four (4)

*27. November

28. Donald Trump

For another way to say this,
see page 25.

29. What is the name of the Vice President of the United States now?

----

30. If the President can no longer serve, who becomes President?

----

31. If both the President and the Vice President can no longer serve, who becomes President?

----

32. Who is the Commander in Chief of the military?

29. Mike Pence

For another way to say this,
see page 25.

30. the Vice President

31. the Speaker of the House

32. the President

33. Who signs bills so they become laws?

----

34. Who can veto bills?

----

35. What does the President's
    Cabinet do?

----

36. What are two Cabinet-level
    positions?

33. the President

34. the President

35. It advises the President.

36. Vice President;
    Secretary of State

    You only need to know 2 positions.
    For other choices, see page 29.

37. What does the judicial branch do?

- -

38. What is the highest court in the United States?

- -

39. How many justices are on the Supreme Court?

- -

40. Who is the Chief Justice of the United States now?

37. It explains laws.

   You need to know one answer.
   For other choices, see page 29.

38. the Supreme Court

39. nine (9)

40. John Roberts

41. Under our Constitution, some powers belong to the federal government What is <u>one</u> power of the federal government?

----

42. Under our Constitution, some powers belong to the states. What is <u>one</u> power of the states?

----

43. Who is the Governor of your state now?

----

*44. What is the capital of your state?

41. to declare war

    You need to know one power.
    For other choices, see page 31.

42. to give a driver's license

    You only need to know one power.
    For more choices, see page 33.

43. Answers will depend on the state you live in.
    If you don't know, ask at your local library or
    go to www.usa.gov.

    [If you live in the District of Columbia you
    should answer that D.C. does not have a
    governor.]

*44. Answers will be different. See page 35.

    [District of Columbia residents should
    answer that D.C. is not a state and does not
    have a capital. Residents of U.S. territories
    should name the capital of the territory.]

*45. What are the two major political
     parties in the United States?

----

46. What is the political party
    of the President now?

----

47. What is the name of the Speaker of
    the House of Representatives?

    [This will change in January 2019. See
    www.lakewoodpublishing.com for the new
    name or ask at a library.]

----

48. There are four amendments to the
    Constitution about who can vote.
    Describe one.

*45. the Democratic Party and
the Republican Party

46. the Republican Party

47. Paul Ryan

48. Any U.S. citizen over 18 years old
can vote.

You need to know one amendment.
For other choices, see page 37.

*49. What is one responsibility that is only for United States citizens?

----

50. Name one right only for United States citizens.

----

51. What are two rights of everyone living in the United States?

----

52. What do we show loyalty to when we say the Pledge of Allegiance?

*49. to serve on a jury

You only need to know one answer.
For other choices, see page 37.

50. to vote in a U.S. election

51. Freedom of speech.
The right to a trial by jury.

For more choices, see page 39.

52. the United States

53. What is one promise you make when you become a United States citizen?

----

*54. How old do citizens have to be to vote for President?

----

55. What are two ways that Americans can participate in their democracy?

----

*56. When is the last day you can send in federal income tax forms?

53. to defend the U.S.

You need to know one answer.
For more choices, see page 41.

*54. At least 18 years old (eighteen and older)

55. (1) vote;
(2) join a political party

For more choices, see page 41.

*56. April 15

57. When must all men register for the Selective Service?

- -

58. What is one reason colonists came to America?

- -

59. Who lived in America before the Europeans arrived?

- -

60. What group of people was taken to America by force and sold as slaves?

57. at age eighteen (18)

58. for freedom

You need to know one reason.
For more reasons, see page 43.

59. American Indians

For another way to say it, see page 45.

60. people from Africa

61. Why did the colonists fight the British?
(Know one reason.)

----

62. Who wrote the Declaration of Independence?

----

63. When was the Declaration of Independence
adopted?

----

64. There were 13 original states.

Name three.

61. because of high taxes
    ("taxation without representation")

    You need to know one answer.
    For other choices, see page 45.

62. Thomas Jefferson

63. July 4, 1776

64. New York
    New Jersey
    North Carolina

    For a complete list, see page 47.

65. What happened at the Constitutional
    Convention ?
    (Know one way to say it.)

----

66. When was the Constitution written?

----

67. The Federalist Papers supported the
    passage of the U.S. Constitution.
    Name one of the writers.

----

68. What is one thing Benjamin Franklin is
    famous for?

65. The Constitution was written.

66. 1787

67. (James) Madison

You need to know one writer.
For other choices, see page 31.

68. He started the first free libraries

You need to know one answer.
For more choices, see page 32.

69. Who is the "Father of Our Country"?

----

*70. Who was the first President?

----

71. What territory did the United States buy from France in 1803?

----

72. Name one war fought by the United States in the 1800s.

69. (George) Washington

*70. (George) Washington

71. Louisiana

For another way to say this,
see page 32.

72. the Civil War

You need to know one war.
For more choices, see page 33.

73. Name the U.S. war between the North and the South.

----

74. Name one problem that led to the Civil War.

----

*75. What was one important thing that Abraham Lincoln did?

----

76. What did the Emancipation Proclamation do?

73. the Civil War

For another way to say this, see page 33.

74. slavery

You need to know one answer.
For other choices, see page 33.

*75. He freed the slaves.

You need to know one answer.
For other choices, see page 33.

76. It freed the slaves

You need to know one answer. For
another choice, see page 34.

77. What did Susan B. Anthony do?

----

*78. Name one war fought by the United
     States in the 1900s.

----

79. Who was President during World War I?

----

80. Who was President during the Great
    Depression and World War II?

77.   She fought for women's rights

You need to know one answer. For
another choice, see page 34.

*78.   World War I

You need to know one answer. For more
choices, see page 34.

79.   (Woodrow) Wilson

80.   Franklin Roosevelt

81. Who did the United States fight
    in World War II?

- -

82. Before he was President, Eisenhower
    was a general. What war was he in?

- -

83. During the Cold War, what was the
    main concern of the United States?

- -

84. What movement tried to end racial
    discrimination?

81. Japan, Germany, and Italy

82. World War II

83. Communism

84. the civil rights movement

*85. What did Martin Luther King, Jr. do?

----

86. What major event happened on September 11, 2001, in the United States?

----

87. Name one American Indian tribe in the United States.

----

88. Name one of the two longest rivers in the United States.

*85. He worked for equality for
all Americans

You need to know one answer. For
other ways to answer, see page 35.

86. Terrorists attacked the United States.

87. Pueblo

You need to know <u>one</u> tribe.
For more tribes, see page 36.

88. Missouri (River)

You need to know one river.
For the other river, see page 36.

89. What ocean is on the West Coast of the United States?

- -

90. What ocean is on the East Coast of the United States?

- -

91. Name one U.S. territory

- -

92. Name one state that borders Canada.

89. Pacific (Ocean)

90. Atlantic (Ocean)

91. Puerto Rico

   You need to know one territory.
   To see the complete list, see page 37.

92. Alaska

   You need to know one state.
   To see the complete list, see page 37.

93. Name one state that borders Mexico.

- -

*94. What is the capital of the
     United States?

- -

*95. Where is the Statue of Liberty?

- -

96. Why does the flag have 13 stripes?

93. California

You need to know one state.
To see a complete list, see page 37.

*94. Washington, D.C.

*95. New York Harbor

You need to know one answer.
For other ways to answer, see page 38.

96. The stripes represent the original 13 colonies.

*97. Why does the flag have 50 stars?

----

98. What is the name of the national anthem?

----

*99. When do we celebrate Independence Day?

----

100. Name two national U.S. holidays.

*97. The stars represent the 50 U.S. states.

For other ways to say this, see page 38

98. "The Star-Spangled Banner"

*99. July 4

100. -Thanksgiving
     - Christmas

You need to know two holidays.
For the complete list, see page 39.

Made in the USA
Las Vegas, NV
07 April 2023

70297719R00098